THE NEXT HORSEMAN

a comedy script for video chat
by Allison Williams

CORIANDER PRESS

Other Plays by Allison Williams:
THE HUNCHBACK OF NOTRE DAME (a musical)
THE TALE OF TSURU
PANTALONE RIDES AGAIN
THE TAMING OF PANTALONE
TRUE STORY (monologue/ensemble)
SUNDAY AT THE MET

Available from Theatrefolk:
HAMLETTE
MMMBETH
THE SCARLET HEART
DROP DEAD, JULIET
POSTCARDS FROM SHAKESPEARE
DEAD MEN DON'T DO RADIO PLAYS

Available from Youthplays:
EVERYBODY COMES TO TIM'S

Available from Playscripts.com:
MISS KENTUCKY

THE NEXT HORSEMAN

© 2020 Allison Williams

CAUTION: This play is fully protected under the copyright laws of the United States and all other countries of the Universal Copyright Convention and is subject to royalty. Changes to the script are expressly forbidden without written consent of the author. Rights to produce, film, or record, in whole or in part, in any medium or in any language, by any group amateur or professional, are fully reserved.

Interested persons are requested to apply for amateur or professional rights to:

Allison K Williams

allison@idowords.net

No part of this script covered by the copyrights hereon may be reproduced or used in any form or by any means—graphic, electronic or mechanical—without the prior written permission of the author. Any request for photocopying, recording, or videotaping in any format or for any platform shall be directed in writing to the author at the address above.

ISBN-13 | 978-1-945736-07-0 (eBook)
ISBN-13 | 978-1-945736-08-7 (paperback)

PRODUCTION NOTE

This play is designed to be flexible! If you are doing it in one class period with little rehearsal, don't worry about props or costumes. Famine can nibble at a bag of chips or veggie sticks rather than the food listed.

If you have time for more of a project, and your actors have the resources, it can be fun to make Death's scythe out of cardboard, Mosquitoes' eyes from an egg carton, record the sounds of the video game and the crying baby, etc. **Scale up or down as your resources and time allow.**

For the **Candidates,** use as many or as few actors as you like, given your cast size and video/audio conference capabilities. Double- or triple-casting works just fine.

CHARACTERS

6 single-cast roles, and 3-13+ actors in roles suitable for doubling.

All characters may be played by any gender.

The Four Horsemen of the Apocalypse
DEATH, formal
FAMINE, hungry
WAR, looking for a fight
PESTILENCE, over it

Assistants
KAY, not quite who they seem to be
CEE, learning the job

Candidates
EXTORTION, a mobster
INTERNET TROLLING, with gamer goggles and Doritos
HUMAN TRAFFICKING, in farmer's hat
AIRPORT SECURITY, in uniform
BIGOTRY, multiple actors of different genders, races and/or ethnicities
CLIMATE CHANGE, a VSCO girl or E-Boy
CONSPIRACY THEORIES, in tinfoil hat
MOSQUITOES, wearing wings
MANSPLAINING, in jacket and tie
BARE FEET IN PUBLIC SPACES, tank top and no shoes
WHITE RAPPERS, exactly like it sounds
INEQUALITY, dressed like the 1%
SCREAMING BABIES ON AIRPLANES, a harried parent with diaper bag and lifelike doll that cries, or crying sound effect

SETTING

A Zoom meeting, Google Hangout or other online video chat, or a telephone conference call. Gestures and actions are if actors are visible—**feel free to adapt stage directions to your technical capabilities and actual surroundings.**

When characters "appear" and "vanish" they can turn their camera on/off, put a piece of paper over the camera, or sit back quietly and pay attention to the main action. The CANDIDATES can either all appear at once, then exit as indicated, or they can appear and exit as indicated.

It's important that FAMINE's desk or table has been wiped clean, thoroughly rinsed, and is safe to eat food directly from the surface. If needed, cover the surface with several layers of plastic wrap (taped in place so it doesn't move around). Their keyboard and any desktop devices should be covered with a layer of plastic wrap.

Famine also needs a tarp or shower curtain under their chair and desk to catch food scraps, and any pets should be kept out of the room. If the actor has allergies/sensitivities, any safe foods may be substituted for those listed.

For Famine's mayonnaise jar, fill a clean, empty mayonnaise jar with white yogurt or vanilla pudding. You could also use a jar of "barbecue sauce" made of chocolate pudding thinned with water plus red food coloring.

TIME

December 31, 2018

THE NEXT HORSEMAN

A video chat window. First Assistant, KAY pops up, dressed as an administrative assistant, reaching for controls/buttons, and stacking paperwork.

KAY: OK, let me just...

Second Assistant, CEE pops up. CEE is a little disheveled but resolute. CEE looks into camera and smooths hair.

CEE: Am I here?

KAY: You're here. You're the new recruit?

CEE: Cee. I'm Cee.

KAY: Welcome, and Happy New Year.

CEE: Thanks! Isn't it kind of weird to meet on New Year's Eve?

KAY: We work a lot of holidays here.

CEE: Headquarters said you needed back-up. I've never been undercover before.

KAY: You've got to really believe you're the second administrative assistant. It's all paperwork. *(pats a stack on her desk)* Think paperwork, eat paperwork, sleep paperwork. Since it's your first day, just take the best notes you can and we'll go over them together afterwards.

CEE: Isn't there a transcript? Like, automatically?

KAY: They're very old-school. Which is great, because we send the encrypted meeting minutes Upstairs for mission planning.

CEE: How did you get into this job? Does anyone know you're—

KAY: Deep cover, Cee. Not a word.

CEE: You can trust me.

KAY *(looks around, leans into camera)*: Infiltration hasn't been easy, but once we know their plans—Oh, stand by.

ASSISTANTS look attentive and as if they are taking notes throughout.

DEATH pops up, wearing a hooded robe (or hoodie) and/or Dia De Los Muertos-style makeup. A scythe is propped against a chair or in view behind Death.

DEATH: Good evening everyone and Happy New Year in— *(checks phone)*—thirty minutes. Thank you all for jumping on our twenty-first century strategy call and apologies that we're eighteen years late. Then again, I'm always late. *(waits for laugh, doesn't get it)* Well. The twentieth century was good, but I think this next hundred years we're going to make a killing. Pestilence?

PESTILENCE pops up, dressed in "home sick today" clothes like a onesie or pajamas, with straggly hair. PESTILENCE might also wear a variety of disease-support ribbons and rubber bracelets. Pestilence sneezes into open hand, examines the output, and wipes hand on own shoulder. If not visible, Pestilence coughs and makes a hawking-spit sound.

PESTILENCE: I need to finish in a hard ten, OK? I think I've got strep throat. And tuberculosis.

Pestilence sets a box of tissues on their table.

DEATH: Famine, are you in the meeting?

FAMINE pops up, making chewing sounds. Famine wears a bib and eats continuously.

FAMINE: Did you guys get the snacks I sent?

WAR pops up, dressed in camouflage, gamer goggles or tinted glasses on. The sound of a loud first-person shooter game fills the audio. If visible, War has a mace or battleaxe strapped to their chair or tucked beside them.

WAR: Snacks? You sent snacks?

KAY *(cutting through, but sweetly)*: Excuse me, War, could you please mute your mic?

WAR: Hang on...*(lifts goggles/glasses, presses something and the noise stops)* First day in the game and I already killed the raccoon, looted all the shops and burned the island to the ground.

CEE: You're playing Animal Crossing?

KAY: Shhh.

WAR: Yo, Famine, where's the snacks?

FAMINE waves a yogurt or hummus or other small food item that's a smooshy substance in a container.

FAMINE: I sent a delivery...

PESTILENCE: Well I didn't get anything.

FAMINE: It was hummus and pita, Doritos and bleu cheese dip, and strawberry smoothies. Oh, and those pink fluffy marshmallow things Death likes.

DEATH: I received a box. It was a coffin filled with falafel and kale.

WAR puts box of leafy greens on desk—if no prop, make first sentence "Famine, you sent that?"

WAR: Famine, you sent this? I thought it was a prank. Like the Trojan Horse—you think it's a cool gift until you open it up, and then boom, you've got Greeks and constipation.

FAMINE *(eating)*: Huh. Weird.

PESTILENCE: Hard ten, gang. *(blows nose, inspects contents of tissue)* I have a pediatrician's waiting room that's not going to infect itself.

DEATH gently thumps phone on desk as if banging a gavel.

DEATH: This meeting is now called to order.

WAR: Yo Death, where's your big hourglass?

DEATH *(shows phone)*: I have an app now.

WAR: Movin' with the times!

DEATH: I am all about time. Or lack thereof. *(waits for laugh, doesn't get it)* Ahem. First topic, transportation. Kay?

KAY *(reading from document or shares screen with graph)*: Stabling fees have increased this year two hundred and fifty percent and horse feed costs have doubled due to worldwide drought.

FAMINE: Sorry guys, it's the cost of doing business.

PESTILENCE: Why do we still have horses, anyway? *(coughs open-mouthed)* Can't we get some e-scooters?

WAR: E-scooters? Who's ever heard of a War E-Scooter? *(grabs a piece of kale and waves it, or gestures grandly)* When Richard the Third strode forth, did he call for his e-scooter? An e-scooter, an e-scooter, my kingdom for an e-scooter?

PESTILENCE: It was the Middle Ages, e-scooters hadn't been invented yet. Move with the times, people.

PESTILENCE wipes nose on sleeve.

DEATH: Some of us still believe in tradition, Pestilence. If a horse was good enough for my father and his father, then a horse is good enough for me. Vote for horses?

WAR: Aye.

FAMINE: They're delicious.

FAMINE reaches bottom of food container, turns it upside down, goes in with a finger for the last bits.

PESTILENCE: Whatever.

CEE: Motion passes, recorded.

KAY: Thank you, Cee.

DEATH: Everyone OK with a thirty-five percent increase in the transportation budget?

WAR: I salute that budget!

PESTILENCE *(sneezes)*: Ah-sure!

FAMINE: Gimme more.

FAMINE begins to make a complicated sandwich like an artisan, lining up cold cuts with bread corners, etc, or starts diving into a bag of junk food.

DEATH: Let's move on to the peer evaluations.

PESTILENCE: Wait, what?

DEATH: Kay sent them out at the turn of the century and is expecting them back this week. I trust eighteen years was long enough for a full report?

If visible, EVERYONE except PESTILENCE holds up a file or sheaf of papers, otherwise, sound of rustling papers is heard.

PESTILENCE: How come you all have paperwork? Kay, where's my paperwork?

KAY: I'm sorry, I was directed not to—

DEATH *(cutting her off)*: War and Famine, superior work. Well executed.

WAR: I set 'em up and hunger knocks 'em down!

FAMINE: Gobble-gobble!

DEATH: Pestilence, your numbers are a grave concern.

PESTILENCE *(defensively)*: Hey, it was a tough century. You saw the plan—it was sick! How was I supposed to know some like, bread mold, was gonna run me down? I threw everything at them! Kay, what were the polio numbers?

CEE shuffles madly through paperwork while KAY promptly holds up a document or shares screen with a graph.

KAY: Fifty-eight thousand cases, but only three thousand deaths.

CEE *(relieved to find the right document)*: Global vaccinations at eighty-five percent.

WAR: Yeah, that's not coming back any time soon.

PESTILENCE *(indicates red ribbon on chest)*: What was wrong with AIDS? It had great potential! Everyone said it was incurable!

DEATH: And yet thirty years later, there's a cure.

PESTILENCE: It could flare up again!

DEATH screen shares or holds up a chart showing decreasing death rates from pandemics.

DEATH: Black death, smallpox, the "great plagues"—they weren't even naming them anymore—

PESTILENCE: They were <u>great</u> plagues!

DEATH: Cholera—One doctor removes the handle from one water pump and poof, a promising epidemic snuffed out.

FAMINE: Where's the fear? Where's the panic? I mean, it's great that you keep rebranding Influenza, but you gotta reinvent yourself.

If visible, FAMINE sticks toothpicks or flags into the now-very-tall sandwich and begins strategizing how to get their mouth around it. If no sandwich, FAMINE roots at the bottom of the junk food bag for crumbs/Cheetos dust/etc.

WAR: What's gonna be next? New Flu? Flu Zero? Followed a few months later by Flu Classic?

PESTILENCE: I've got plenty of new ideas. My next outbreak's going to be incredible. Have you seen Planet of the Apes?

WAR: Did it have lasers?

PESTILENCE: Think "Ape-ocalypse"!

DEATH: Your time has passed, Pestilence. We're voting you out of the Horsemen.

PESTILENCE: Really? After years of tireless service, you throw me away like a used bedpan? Oh, Phil in Marketing is going to love this. How's he going to sell the Three Horsemen of the Apocalypse? Talk about rebranding! That's gonna suck up the advertising budget for a millennium!

WAR: Yeah, well, we thought about that. We're having try-outs today.

DEATH: You may sit in, if you like. In a strictly non-executive capacity.

CEE: Excuse me? *(nervously, reading from a paper)* Uh, Pestilence? Please make sure company-issued horse is washed and returned in the same condition in which you received it.

DEATH: To be clear, we want a <u>white</u> horse back.

PESTILENCE: You're taking away Mr. Whinny?

DEATH: Perhaps for your retirement present we'll get you a nice e-scooter. Just stay out of traffic—I'm reaping great rewards from those things in major cities.

WAR: They're basically death-skateboards.

FAMINE: Uh, Pestilence, on a personal note, I'd just like to say...dibs on your parking space. Right next to the exit! *(pumps fist)* Sweet!

FAMINE returns attention to sandwich, attempts to take a bite, sandwich explodes over desk. Famine begins eating sandwich components directly from the desk, including licking up condiments (see note re setting). If no sandwich, FAMINE rips open snack bag and begins licking the inside.

PESTILENCE: I can't believe you guys. This is nauseating! I've been infectious since the beginning. As soon as more than two of them got together, I was doing my thing. And where are you getting these so-called "candidates"? Did you run an ad in the paper? Is there some job board I've never seen?

WAR: We have an agency. They're actually very good.

FAMINE: Don't be so bitter. We'll all be out of a job one day.

DEATH: Not me.

FAMINE: It's not like you haven't had time to save up for retirement.

PESTILENCE: I'm not some tottering senior citizen, I'm barely 7000 years old! Why should I be the one getting early retirement? *(for UK, "pensioner")*

WAR: Remember when the first humans used to walk hundreds of miles to find the right rocks to make fire, and spear points? Then somebody discovered bronze and poof, outta business!

PESTILENCE: I'm just having a slump! I'll be back. And when it happens…better make sure you buy shares in bananas. Ape. Ocalypse.

FAMINE *(stops eating to talk)*: You're done, Pestilence. Those guys who made armor, until everyone realized how dumb it was to try and fight in a two-hundred-pound metal suit? Gone the way of the dodo.

DEATH: And we all know what happened to the dodo. *(smiles and caresses scythe)* Yes, it's a rich tapestry of progress, ending inevitably in extinction. But through it all, we prevail. Remember our company motto:

DEATH, FAMINE, WAR and a half-hearted PESTILENCE: As long as humans are mean, selfish, cruel and cowardly, there will always be work for us!

DEATH: If it were up to me, I'd never have moved past the Dark Ages. But times change, and so must we. Let's get these candidates in—we've got a long list and I'm expecting the cable guy sometime between noon and next July.

FAMINE: What's broken?

DEATH: Nothing. He's on my list and I'm trying to work from home.

WAR: Hold on, before we attack this, what's the selection criteria? Is it fight to the death and winner takes all, or panel interviews?

KAY: Excuse me, Jerry in HR has issued a new policy against fighting to the death.

WAR: Sometimes I wonder if Jerry's really in tune with the ethos of our organization.

DEATH: Good point. Kay, make a note to have Jerry peeled and skewered. Is he working from home?

KAY: I believe so.

DEATH: Well, send someone over from the peeling department.

KAY: Noted. *(makes a note)*

FAMINE sets out a large mayonnaise jar and several spoons of varying sizes. When the set-up is finished, Famine begins eating spoonfuls of 'mayonnaise' directly from the jar.

DEATH: And, uh, new assistant?

CEE *(startled to be called on)*: Yes? Yes! I'm Cee.

DEATH: I want it minuted that all recruitment processes next century have a mandatory fight to the death.

CEE: Do you want that at the beginning or as a final stage?

DEATH: Put it at the start. Then we'll save time in the interview round.

KAY: If you're ready, I'll patch in the first candidates? You each have a scoring sheet, please rank each candidate on a scale of seventeen, with eight being the highest score.

FAMINE: Who the heck makes a scoring system of seventeen?

KAY: I believe it was Jerry in HR.

DEATH: Jerry! OK, after the peeling and the skewering, cancel his gym membership and destroy his key to the executive washroom. In fact, make it a rule he can only use the washroom after Pestilence has been in there.

PESTILENCE: Admit it, dysentery's always a classic.

DEATH: Kay, may I make a general announcement?

KAY: Just a moment. Everyone, your candidate lists are in your packets.

PESTILENCE: The packet I didn't get?

Candidates appear: EXTORTION, INTERNET TROLLING, HUMAN TRAFFICKING , AIRPORT SECURITY, BIGOTRY (multiple people), CLIMATE CHANGE, CONSPIRACY THEORIES, MOSQUITOES, MANSPLAINING, BARE FEET IN PUBLIC SPACES, WHITE RAPPERS, INEQUALITY, SCREAMING BABIES ON AIRPLANES.

KAY: Go ahead, boss.

DEATH: Thank you all for being here today and for your interest in the proud tradition of the Four Horsemen of the Apocalypse. I hope you all found the location inconvenient and the parking impossible.

CEE: Security is issuing tickets and booting cars right now. You can pay at the impound lot.

DEATH: Before you ask, no we don't validate parking. By the way, is Extortion here?

EXTORTION *(New Jersey accent)*: Right here, buddy.

DEATH: Good work.

EXTORTION: Happy to be part of the family. You know, if you could see your way to promoting me up to the horseman level, we won't have to talk about that garment factory incident in Bangladesh...

WAR: Whoa!

DEATH: No need to revisit that.

FAMINE: I wasn't the project lead.

PESTILENCE: I wasn't even there!

EXTORTION: Yeah, it'd sure be a shame if Upstairs heard about that one. Aren't you supposed to wait until the building collapses on its own?

DEATH: It was one lousy load-bearing beam. Kay?! *(signals 'cut him off!')*

KAY *(sweetly)*: I'm sorry, Extortion, I think there's a problem with your connection...

KAY punches a button. EXTORTION vanishes from the call/video.

FAMINE *(Speaks unintelligibly through a mouthful of food, then swallows)*: Ahem. For those of you unfamiliar with the panel interview format, it's kind of like X-Factor *(use name of popular TV talent competition)*. Candidates with little or no talent, having failed multiple times, seize a last-gasp opportunity to make something of themselves by sharing their innermost private lives, even though they stand zero chance of succeeding without a bunch of contrived support, ending ultimately in humiliation.

DEATH: It's exactly like X-Factor. *(same substitution)*

WAR: This process lets us see how you respond under stressful and challenging conditions. You need to sell yourselves to us! Not literally, Human Trafficking.

HUMAN TRAFFICKING has pint of berries or small pyramid of tomatoes on desk.

HUMAN TRAFFICKING: But that's where I shine! Like the reflection in the hunted eyes of a worker whose boss took their passport.

FAMINE: Guess this job's not for you. Can you get me some of those strawberries?

HUMAN TRAFFICKING *(huffy)*: Fine.

HUMAN TRAFFICKING vanishes.

WAR: This is so lame! Can't we just throw them all in a pit with a couple of machetes?

DEATH: Kay, make a note to have Jerry slowly barbecued.

KAY: Dry rub or sauce?

DEATH: Low-cal ranch dressing.

HORSEMEN, CANDIDATES and ASSISTANTS all recoil in disgust.

FAMINE: Even I won't eat that.

DEATH: No-one said the job would be easy. Speaking of disgusting, Internet Trolling?

INTERNET TROLLING *(a casual cheer)*: Q-Anon, Four-Chan, Eight-Chan, a dollar, I'm gonna dox you, so stand up and holler!

DEATH: I love your enthusiasm, but your comments on the application were out of order.

INTERNET TROLLING: You said you wanted the lowest of the low!

DEATH: And yet you don't even reach that bar. You're excused.

INTERNET TROLLING: I know where you live! And in five minutes, so will all of Twitter!

WAR: Are you threatening the Four Horsemen of the Apocalypse?

INTERNET TROLLING: I taped this call! It's going on YouTube!

KAY: Ending your call, Trolling.

INTERNET TROLLING vanishes.

FAMINE: Can we just see the candidates in the order on the sheet?

WAR *(looking at sheet)*: It's not alphabetical...

CEE: It's by descending order of weight, sub-sorted by number of consonants in their name.

DEATH: I know we recruited Jerry for his ability to inflict mental torture, but not on us. Who's first?

KAY: Airport Security. *(no response)* Airport Security. *(no response)* Airport Security?

AIRPORT SECURITY: Reporting for duty and ready to scan.

DEATH: Didn't you hear your name?

AIRPORT SECURITY: Don't rush me. You shoulda gotten here earlier. Look, I'd love to join the team, but Death, we're going to have to switch you to a plastic scythe. War, can you turn off those electronics? Now turn 'em back on again and prove they work. Famine, no drink bottles. Anyone got an embarrassing personal item I can wave around?

PESTILENCE: You think you're gonna replace me with this guy?

WAR: Yeah, I'm not seeing full engagement here.

KAY punches a button. AIRPORT SECURITY vanishes. Sound of crying baby.

WAR: Ugh, who's that?

KAY: Screaming Babies on Airplanes, you're in the meeting.

SCREAMING BABIES ON AIRPLANES *(if visible, holds baby doll)*: Sorry I'm late, Airport Security was parked in front of me. I just need to change a diaper on this tray table, one second.

FAMINE: Ew, gross!

PESTILENCE: Some things are too disgusting even for me.

WAR: Aren't you really just an annoyance?

SCREAMING BABIES ON AIRPLANES: I make people angry, then they get off the flight and make terrible business decisions. Oh, and I can really support Pestilence. You should see this little fellow sneeze. Want to see him projectile vomit? It goes three rows!

EVERYONE: No!

KAY: Ending your call.

SCREAMING BABIES ON AIRPLANES vanishes.

WAR: Do we have any serious candidates? Or are you all just something that bothers people?

CEE: White Rappers, are you here?

WHITE RAPPERS appears.

WHITE RAPPERS: I see you dawg, I'm in the house to make strife, you see me, you know it, I'm endin' yo' life.

DEATH: Next.

WHITE RAPPERS vanishes.

KAY: Bare Feet in Public Spaces?

BARE FEET IN PUBLIC SPACES appears, bare feet up on their desk and as fully in camera as possible.

BARE FEET IN PUBLIC SPACES: Trackin' germs around like a pro!

WAR: We just fired Pestilence, we don't need another biological weapon.

BARE FEET IN PUBLIC SPACES: That's cool. Anybody mind if I vape?

EVERYONE: Yes!

BARE FEET IN PUBLIC SPACES vanishes.

KAY: Mosquitoes?

PESTILENCE: What?!

MOSQUITOES appears, wearing wings and large sunglasses or two parts of a clear egg carton as "insect eyes."

MOSQUITOES: I'd like to—zzzzzzz—share my achievements in Malaria, Yellow Fever—zzzz—Zika and Chikungunya. *(chicken-gun-ya)*

PESTILENCE: Are you kidding me, you parasite? You're taking credit for my projects in front of my face?

MOSQUITOES: Oh, hi, Pestilence...I thought they fired you.

PESTILENCE: Do I look fired?

WAR: Fired up.

PESTILENCE: Mosquitoes, hah! Without me, you're barely an annoyance. *(baby voice)* Oh, I'm itchy! *(serious)* They can deal with you with a newspaper. You can't even fly if they turn on a fan. I made you and I can break you, my friend.

MOSQUITOES: We're zzz—still friends?

PESTILENCE: We're not even frenemies. And don't mistake silence for weakness ever again! Buzz off!

MOSQUITOES vanishes.

FAMINE: Wow, ripped out the soul, devastated the self-esteem, with a side of cruelty and vindictiveness! Nice work, Pestilence. *(toasts Pestilence with a bottle and drinks)*

PESTILENCE: All of a sudden my "Ape-ocalypse" doesn't sound so bad, does it?

DEATH: Ahem. Are we down to the serious candidates, Kay?

KAY: Yes, boss. Do we have Inequality?

INEQUALITY *(very corporate)*: Yes? I'm going to need a company laptop, a wardrobe allowance, and my own assistant.

DEATH: I'm afraid we don't usually—

INEQUALITY: And a salary 50% higher than anyone else in the same job.

DEATH: But you have identical qualifications.

INEQUALITY: Well, if everyone else had the same thing, it wouldn't be inequality anymore.

FAMINE *(sets whipped-cream pie on desk)*: Sounds reasonable. Nothing better than the whole pie! *(begins eating the pie face-first)*

PESTILENCE: That's all you've got? Inequality is so obvious! All you do is make unfair things sound reasonable. Any idiot can defeat Inequality if they put some effort into it. It's just reverse envy.

INEQUALITY: Like reverse racism?

PESTILENCE: That's not a thing!

INEQUALITY: Whoa, calm down there, nobody's going to listen if you're yelling.

DEATH: Sorry, but you just don't seem like a team player.

INEQUALITY *(gestures to self)*: Duh! Inequality!

WAR: Don't get me wrong, you're a solid enabler, but you're not really Horseman calibre. You're more of a wingman. You handle set-up, then bring us in and we get the job done. But we already have a whole Wingmen department. Do we need any more tactical support? Can we get a report from Wingmen?

CEE *(trying to make a note)*: Sorry, I'm still getting to know everyone. Who manages that department?

KAY: That's Steve.

CEE: Evil Steve or the other Steve?

KAY: The other Steve. Evil Steve is away on paternity leave.

DEATH: Thank you, Inequality. We'll be in touch if anything opens up in Wingmen.

INEQUALITY vanishes.

WAR: Is Stupidity here? He killed it in the pre-interview.

FAMINE *(covered in pie, waves phone)*: Stupidity texted. He couldn't find the building. *(grabs a towel and wipes face)*

WAR: How about Conspiracy Theories?

CONSPIRACY THEORIES appears, wearing tinfoil hat and Lizard People t-shirt.

CONSPIRACY THEORIES: Hi. Nostradamus predicted I wouldn't get this job, because you're all controlled by the government. Which is both incredibly far-reaching and controlling and also completely incompetent.

DEATH: And your passion is...?

CONSPIRACY THEORIES: I dream up unlikely and unfeasible scenarios and then people convince each other they're actually true.

WAR: How is that any different than Lying? Or Paranoia?

CONSPIRACY THEORIES: It's not. I just have a better agent. Would you like to hear about the Illuminati?

EVERYONE: No!

CONSPIRACY THEORIES: Um, thanks for your time. Is Social Media still here? She's my ride.

CONSPIRACY THEORIES vanishes.

KAY: Bigotry?

BIGOTRY appears. They are several people, ideally of differing genders, races, and national origins. Lines should be divided as if they are a chorus.

BIGOTRY *(ad-lib)*: Hi, hello, how's it going. *(etc)*

WAR: You're all bigotry? Are you like a squad? Because we've only got the one horse. You'll have to take turns walking.

PESTILENCE: It wouldn't be an issue if we had e-scooters.

BIGOTRY: I am a multi-faceted, omni-transformational, manifestation of a pseudo-entity.

FAMINE: Huh?

WAR: Slow your roll, Mister Dictionary.

BIGOTRY: I come in all shapes, sizes and colours. I hate Blacks, Asians, Jews, Muslims, Whites, Catholics, Protestants, Socialists, Capitalists, Fascists, Antifa, and anyone who isn't exactly the same as me. You can also call me Sexism, Ageism, Discrimination, Xenophobia and Mansplaining.

DEATH: You forgot Racism.

BIGOTRY: I don't see color.

CEE: I have a record of Racism working in Human Resources? He was fired last century.

FAMINE: Oh yeah—not a team player.

WAR: He was all over the place.

DEATH: Ah, Bigotry, you do realize no two people in the world are exactly alike?

BIGOTRY: What do you think has kept me in business so long? I really think I can be a valued member of the team.

FAMINE: I like them. Bigotry, do you have any questions for us?

BIGOTRY: Where exactly do you come from?

DEATH: The collective unconscious. We're archetypes of the challenges facing humankind.

BIGOTRY: Male or female?

MANSPLAINING: Well, actually, as archetypical entities manifested from human consciousness, they don't have gender.

BIGOTRY: We all know that, Mansplaining.

MANSPLAINING: I was just saying.

BIGOTRY: Do you have a birth certificate or a passport that can prove your origins?

DEATH: What?

BIGOTRY: It's just that you look kind of different and I find that disturbing.

DEATH: Thank you, Bigotry. Please email Kay with your resume.

All of BIGOTRY vanishes.

DEATH: I really like them, but I don't see them all fitting on that horse. Who's next?

KAY: Climate Change.

PESTILENCE: Is that even a thing?

FAMINE: Don't you remember? With the robes, and the long grey hair? After that volcano erupted in 1816?

CLIMATE CHANGE appears, dressed as a VSCO girl or E-boy.

CLIMATE CHANGE: What up Horsemen? It's been a minute.

DEATH: You look...different.

CLIMATE CHANGE: It's right in the name, dude. Things start changing, I change with 'em. I wasn't even gonna show up for another fifteen hundred years, but hey, internal combustion and boom! It me!

DEATH: I'm not sure another Ice Age would really be the pivot our organization needs.

CLIMATE CHANGE: Whoa, I'm not just natural catastrophes anymore. Used to be, I'd wait for a volcano or a meteor, then stroll in and do my thing while the smoke clears. Then you four ride in and I go mess up some other planet for a while. Unlike you humanity-destroyers, I don't need living things to do my thing.

FAMINE: That has potential. I gotta ruminate on that.

CLIMATE CHANGE: Have you seen Venus lately? All my own work. Hashtag greenhouse gases!

WAR: I'm getting a solid vibe here. On target.

PESTILENCE: But you're not really a self-starter, are you. You need someone else to give that first push.

CLIMATE CHANGE: Jealous much?

PESTILENCE: Hey, I'm sure you're awesome when you're in the zone, but can we really count on humanity to keep you fully employed?

CLIMATE CHANGE *(makes calming hands gesture)*: Namaste, Pestilence. Or Trauma-stay, as I like to call it. My last couple efforts I was testing my wings, you know? Cool things down and knock off some diplodocuses. *("dip-low-doke-us-es")* Warm it back up again, good-bye glaciers. Now I'm the total package. Before, there were barely enough people on earth for a good rave, but now we got Coachella and seven billion eating, pooping, not cleaning-it-up humans strolling around like *(mocking)* 'I'm bipedal, look at me go.'

(leans in, serious)

Look around, man. How many resources are really left? War, the fighting over arable land is heating up—see what I did there? Famine, I'm your wingman! Water gets saltier, starts drying up...then here comes Big D! You step in and finish it off.

(leans back, confident)

Those are guaranteed numbers, friends. You're gonna be so busy you'll have to start franchising.

WAR: We could deploy one Bigot on every team.

CLIMATE CHANGE: I love that! Way to think outside the box, Fighty McFighter! And if we expand, there's room for everyone, even Germ-Face.

PESTILENCE *(surprised and flattered)*: Thank you...I was actually thinking about going solo, but...

CLIMATE CHANGE: Pestilence, baby, there's no Four Horsemen without you! It's a win, win, win, and I'm waving the checkered flag over all of us!

DEATH: Climate Change, you've been a real eye-opener. We will definitely be in touch. We can reach you through the agency?

CLIMATE CHANGE: And through my Facebook page, Instagram and Tiktok.

WAR: One last thing. It's great to see you in person, but I've received reports that you're...not really genuine?

CLIMATE CHANGE: What, like I'm a narc or something? I'm gonna infiltrate and rat you out to *(points upward)* Upstairs?

KAY and CEE shift and fidget, deeply uncomfortable.

DEATH: No, no. But are you real enough? I certainly admire your work, but you've been rather subtle the past couple hundred years.

CLIMATE CHANGE: Truth and beauty, baby. All part of the plan. By the time they all believe I'm the real deal, it'll be too late to do anything! Oh, and if you bought a condo in Miami, it's sell time, for reals.

DEATH: Kay, call my real estate agent after this.

KAY: Certainly, boss.

CLIMATE CHANGE: No pressure, my horse-pals. Think it over. I'll be supporting your squad whether I'm on the official team or not.

FAMINE: Very gracious.

CLIMATE CHANGE: Ciao!

CLIMATE CHANGE vanishes.

WAR: I think we've got a new Horseman. Veni, Vidi, Victory!

PESTILENCE: Wait!

DEATH *(testy)*: What is it, Pestilence?

PESTILENCE: I've got a great idea for an infection.

FAMINE: Yeah, we've heard that before. Ape-ocalypse.

PESTILENCE: Just hear me out. Look, remember what Climate Change said about no-one believing until it's too late? What if we enlisted Social Media and Conspiracy Theories as support staff, and we do a plague no-one believes in!

WAR: That's got potential...

FAMINE: Where am I on this menu?

PESTILENCE: All the workers get sick, so no-one can pick crops. We put Bigotry on the street team. Keep all those *(sarcastic air quotes)* "foreigners" out and everyone'll be starving in like, four weeks.

WAR: What's my battle plan?

PESTILENCE: They don't believe our plague exists...but it's someone else's fault!

DEATH: That's two directly contradictory ideas.

PESTILENCE: Humans are great at that.

DEATH: All right, Pestilence. Let's put a pin in that. You're back on the team, we recruit Climate Change as a contractor, everyone's got a role. I'll want active contributions on the ideas board. War, get us a report on which countries are reliably belligerent. Pestilence, stay focused on contagion and mortality.

PESTILENCE: On it. *(coughs experimentally)* I think that goes about six feet.

FAMINE: Does this mean I don't get that parking space?

DEATH: You can have Jerry's. Great meeting, team, we'll regroup this time tomorrow. I'll reschedule the cable guy so I'll still have wifi. Have a killer day and Happy 2019!

WAR *(pulls goggles down)*: See you on the battlefield!

FAMINE: I'll bring refreshments!

DEATH, WAR, PESTILENCE and FAMINE vanish. KAY and CEE are the only ones left.

CEE: Wow. That didn't end like I thought it would.

KAY: It's a nimble organization. Are you up for the pace?

CEE: Absolutely. Do you think they suspected me?

KAY: No. You were great. And I need your help. Every time the horsemen start a new project, there's a lot of clean-up to do. We can't stop them, but we can influence the results, if you know what I mean.

CEE: I'm all about change. It only takes a couple of us, right?

KAY: Just a little push in the right place and hold steady. I do my best, but I really need someone with your skills. Welcome to the mission.

CEE: Thanks. Sorry, I didn't get your full name. What should I call you?

KAY: I'm Kindness. But Kay is fine.

CEE: I'm Courage. Call me Cee.

KAY: There's a lot to do. And it's going to take a long time.

CEE: Let's get to work.

END OF PLAY

ACKNOWLEDGEMENTS

The biggest thanks to Alf Pomells for starting the process, contributing ideas, and cover design concept. He refused a co-writing credit, but he deserves one.

And many, many thanks for their help, input and inspiration (on this and many other plays) to Iobel Andemicael, Sky Burr-Drysdale, Todd Avery, Todd Espeland, and especially Mark Daniels and his Weber High School (Utah) students who were my first readers:

Theron Peterson
Marie Sorenson
Tobey Griffeth
Mason Olney
Tanner Linford
Alyssa Shupe

ABOUT THE AUTHOR

Allison Williams holds an MFA from Western Michigan University. She spent 15 years as the Artistic Director of the circus company Aerial Angels and led the creation of FALLEN (Bible women + circus), SLEEPWALKERS (Grand Guignol + circus) and STAND UP 8 (reality circus). Allison still coaches in the school residency program Starfish Circus, which trains 2000 K-12 students every year in circus arts and 21st-Century Skills. (www.starfishcircus.com)

Allison's essays have appeared in the New York Times, and she has told stories on the Moth and Snap Judgment. She has written a YA novel about mental illness, ALL THESE LITTLE STARS, and is working on an adaptation of Oliver Twist, set in present-day New York.

Allison is based in Dubai but home less than 100 days a year, not all at the same time. Find out where she is by following her on Instagram @guerillamemoir – if you're doing her play and she's within 200 miles, she'll probably stop by.

TO PRODUCE THIS PLAY

Royalties are as follows:

Classroom production: $50
- under 30 audience members
- no tickets sold, donations may be accepted
- screen recordings may be shared with family & friends but not more than five minutes' total excerpts may be posted publicly online.
- Includes shareable/copiable PDF for student scripts

Community production: $50
- up to 100 audience members
- donations may be accepted or tickets sold
- not more than five minutes' total excerpts may be posted online for promotional purposes.

Professional production $75
- up to 100 audience members
- donations may be accepted or tickets sold
- screen recording may be used for 7 days for additional viewings.

Get in Touch
- if your production will be viewed by 100+
- if you can't afford the royalties
- if you'd like a class video chat with the playwright

Please PayPal royalties to allison@idowords.net and let us know when your production is.

www.ingramcontent.com/pod-product-compliance
Lightning Source LLC
Chambersburg PA
CBHW030141100526
44592CB00011B/998